NEW HAVEN FREE PUBLIC LIBRARY

3 5000 06788 9609

OFFICIALLY WITHDRAWN
NEW HAVEN FREE PUBLIC LIBRARY

DATE DUE

OCT 05 2005

STETSON LIBRARY

D0906530

NEW HAVEN FREE PUBLIC LIBRARY
133 ELM STREET
NEW HAVEN, CT 06510

SCIENCE STARTERS

Up in the Air

Wendy Madgwick

**RAINTREE
STECK-VAUGHN**
P U B L I S H E R S
The Steck-Vaughn Company

Austin, Texas

Titles in this series:
Up in the Air • Water Play • Magnets and Sparks
Super Sound • Super Materials • Light and Dark
Living Things • On the Move

© Copyright 1999, text, Steck-Vaughn Company

All rights reserved. No part of this book may be reproduced or utilized in any form or by any means, electronic or mechanical, including photocopying, recording, or by any information storage and retrieval system, without permission in writing from the Publisher. Inquiries should be addressed to: Copyright Permissions, Steck-Vaughn Company, P.O. Box 26015, Austin, TX 78755.

Published by Raintree Steck-Vaughn Publishers, an imprint of Steck-Vaughn Company

Library of Congress Cataloging-in-Publication Data
Madgwick, Wendy.
Up in the air / Wendy Madgwick.
     p.   cm.—(Science Starters)
     Includes bibliographical references and index.
     Summary: Provides instructions for a variety of projects that demonstrate the properties and uses of air.
     ISBN 0-8172-5325-4
     1. Air—Experiments—Juvenile literature.
     [1. Air—Experiments. 2. Experiments.]
     I. Title. II. Series: Madgwick, Wendy, Science starters.
     QC161.2.M33   1998
     533'.6—dc21   98-10755

Printed in Italy. Bound in the United States.
1 2 3 4 5 6 7 8 9 0 03 02 01 00 99

Words that appear in **bold** in the text are explained in the glossary on page 30.

Illustrations: Catherine Ward/Simon Girling Associates
Photographer: Andrew Sydenham
Picture Acknowledgments: pages 5, 17, 20 top, 23 Zefa; page 14 Bruce Coleman/Robert P.Carr; page 20 bottom OSF/Paolo Fioratti.

STETSON BRANCH LIBRARY

j533.6
MADGWICK

Contents

Looking at Air

This book has lots of fun activities to help you find out about air. Here are some simple rules you should follow before doing an activity.

- Always tell an adult what you are doing. Ask him or her if you may do the activity.
- Always read through the activity before you begin. Collect all the materials you will need. They are listed on page 28.
- Watch what happens carefully. Some things happen quickly, but others take a long time.
- Make sure you have enough space to set up your activity.
- Follow the steps carefully. Ask an adult to help you cut things.
- Keep a notebook. Draw pictures or write down what you did and what happened.
- Always clear up when you have finished. Wash your hands.

▶ The air inside these balloons is heated by burners. Hot air rises and lifts the balloons.

Air? Where?

Air is all around us. But we cannot see it. We cannot taste it or touch it. So how do we know it is there? Let's find out.

Blow it out

Put your hand in front of your mouth. Now pucker your lips and blow. What can you feel? You can feel the air blowing on your hand, but you cannot see it.

Note: The materials you will need for this project and all the activities in this book are listed on Page 28.

Fan it

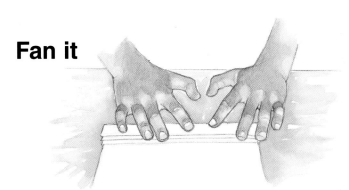

1 Take a sheet of paper. Fold over one side. Turn the paper over. Fold again.

2 Keep on turning and folding the paper. Tape or staple one end.

3 Wave your fan in front of your face. Can you feel the air moving?

Bubbles

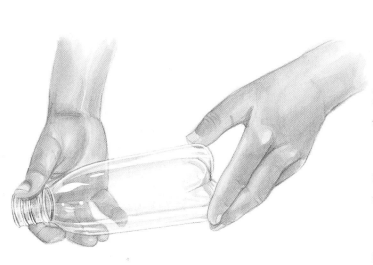

2 Fill a bowl with water. Push the bottle under the water. Watch.

1 Take an empty bottle. What is in it?

Can you see bubbles coming out? They are bubbles of air. The water going into the bottle forced the air out. This is because air takes up space and is all around you.

Weigh It Up

Air is all around us. It takes up space. But does it weigh anything? How can you find out?

How do you blow up balloons?
You pump air into them.

When you pump air into a balloon
it gets bigger, or **inflates**.
What happens when you let the air out?
The balloon gets smaller,
or **deflates**.

Light as air

We can weigh air, using two balloons.

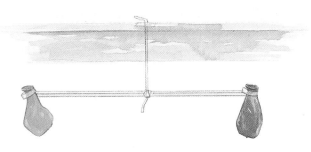

1 Mark the middle of a long stick.

3 Cut two pieces of tape the same size. Tape one balloon to each end of the stick. Make sure the stick is still level.

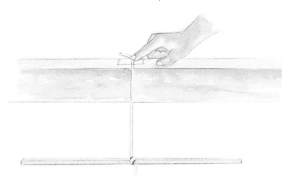

2 Tie a piece of string around the middle of the stick. Tape the other end to the edge of a table. Make sure the stick is level.

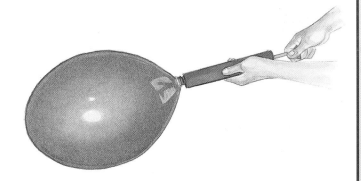

4 Unstick one balloon and blow it up. Ask an adult to tie it.

5 Retape the balloon to the same place on the stick. Does the stick stay level? Which end goes down?

The end with the blown-up balloon will go down. It is heavier than the empty balloon. Air has weight.

Air Power

Like all objects, air is pulled down to the ground by **gravity**. As air is pulled down it presses on things. This is called **air pressure**.

Put a ruler on the table.
Make sure part of it lies over the edge.
Put a sheet of paper on top of the ruler.
Gently hit the end of the ruler.

Does the paper lift up?

Can you feel something
pressing down on the paper?

Air presses down on the paper.

High or low?

Air pressure can tell us about the **weather**. High pressure means good weather. Low pressure means bad weather.

1 Cover a glass with plastic wrap. Tape the plastic wrap in place.

2 Cut one end of a straw into a point. Color the pointer black. Tape the other end to the middle of the plastic wrap.

3 Take another glass. Put the glasses next to each other in a shoe box. Make a card rule with narrow divisions as shown. Tape it to the other glass so that the pointer points to 0. Keep the box away from a window or draft.

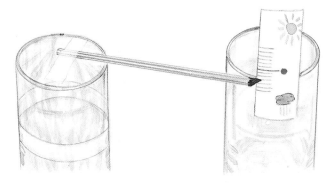

4 Look at the pointer each day. If it moves down, the air pressure is lower.

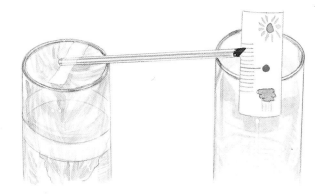

5 If the pointer moves up, the air pressure is higher.

Up, Up, and Away

Warm air takes up more space than cold air.

Warm air is also lighter than cold air.

This means warm air rises.

Blow up

Can warm air blow up a balloon
on its own? Try and see.

1 Stretch a balloon over the end
of a plastic bottle.

2 Hold the bottle in a bowl of warm water.
What happens?

The air inside the bottle gets warmer and
expands, so the balloon inflates.

3 Add lots of ice to the water.
What happens?

The air in the bottle gets
colder and **contracts**, so the
balloon deflates.
Warm air takes up more room
than cold air.

Spinning snakes!

Does hot air rise?

Find out with a snake mobile.

1 Tie thread around the middle of a straw.

2 Draw two snake shapes on a piece of paper. Color and cut out the shapes.

3 Tape thread to the top of each snake.

4 Tape the snakes to either end of the straw.

5 Hang the mobile over a warm radiator, making sure the straw is level. Make another mobile. Hang it in the middle of the room. Which snakes move the most? Warm air rises. This moving air makes the snakes hanging above the warm radiator spin faster.

13

Keep Warm

A warm object cools down if it is in a cold place. Heat from the warm object goes into the cold air. Air can help keep things warm.

This bird is cold. It has fluffed up its feathers to keep warm. Air is caught among its feathers.

Cover up

Collect five jars of the same size (with lids).

1 Wrap a woolen scarf loosely around jar 1.

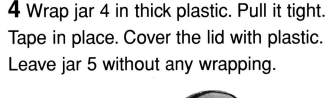

2 Fill a box and lid with crumpled paper. Put jar 2 in the middle.

4 Wrap jar 4 in thick plastic. Pull it tight. Tape in place. Cover the lid with plastic. Leave jar 5 without any wrapping.

3 Wrap thick paper around jar 3. Pull it tight. Tape it in place. Cover the lid with paper.

5 Pour very warm water into each jar. Put on the lids and covers. Cover the lid of jar 1 with the scarf. Put the lid on the box of jar 2. Leave the jars for an hour.

6 Take off the lid of each jar. Test the water with your finger.
The water in jars 1 and 2 should be warmest. The air trapped in the wrappings helped keep the water warm. We call this **insulation**.

On the Move

Moving air does not press on objects as much as still air. It does not have as much pushing power.

Dip it!

Try to blow a piece of paper away. You will need two large books of the same thickness.

2 Place a piece of paper over the books.

3 Blow underneath the paper. What happens to the paper? The paper dips as you blow. The still air above the paper pushes it down.

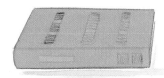

1 Put the books on a table.

Swing it

Can you blow two plastic bricks apart?

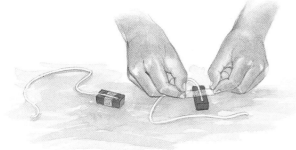

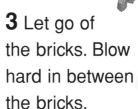

1 Tape some string to two plastic bricks.

3 Let go of the bricks. Blow hard in between the bricks.

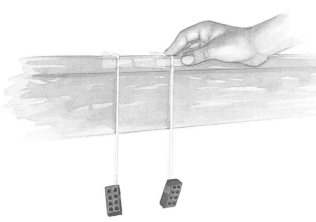

2 Tape the strings to the edge of a table. They should be about 2.5 in. (6 cm) apart. Make sure the bricks swing freely. Hold them still.

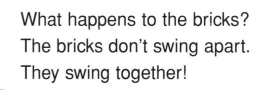

What happens to the bricks? The bricks don't swing apart. They swing together!

A **whirlwind** is a wind that swirls around and around. Twigs, branches, and even trees can get picked up.

Up We Go

Moving air has less pushing power than still air. Flying animals and aircraft use moving air to stay in the air. They all have specially shaped wings.

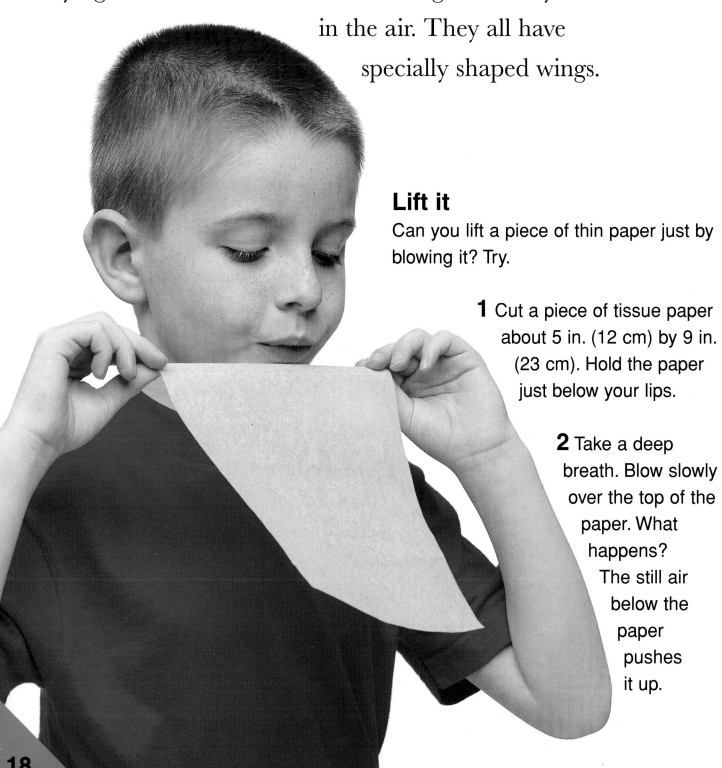

Lift it

Can you lift a piece of thin paper just by blowing it? Try.

1 Cut a piece of tissue paper about 5 in. (12 cm) by 9 in. (23 cm). Hold the paper just below your lips.

2 Take a deep breath. Blow slowly over the top of the paper. What happens? The still air below the paper pushes it up.

Wing power

Does the shape of a wing help it rise? Let's see.

1 Cut two pieces of tissue paper about 8$\frac{1}{2}$ in. (22 cm) by 4 in. (10 cm). Fold them in half with a sharp crease.

2 Tape the edges of one piece of tissue paper together.

3 Take the other piece of paper. Put the top half about $\frac{3}{4}$ in. (2 cm) from the edge of the bottom. Tape in place.

4 Slide a ruler into the straight wing. Hold the ruler about 2 in. (5 cm) in front of your mouth. Take a deep breath. Blow slowly. What happens to the paper wing? It does not rise into the air.

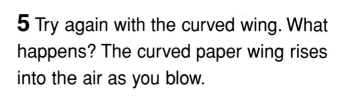

5 Try again with the curved wing. What happens? The curved paper wing rises into the air as you blow.

Let's Fly

Flying animals and aircraft have smooth shapes. This helps them fly well. We say they are **streamlined**.

Look at these pictures.
The bird and plane have smooth shapes. How does this help them fly well? Try this next test and see.

Dart about
Get three pieces of paper
8$\frac{1}{2}$ in. X 11 in. (21$\frac{1}{2}$ cm X 28 cm).

1 Throw one sheet of paper into the air. How well does it fly?

2 Now screw up the paper into a ball. Throw it. How well does it fly?

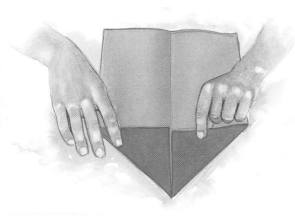

3 Now make a streamlined dart. Fold a piece of paper down the middle. Open the paper. Fold over the top corners. Make sure they meet in the middle.

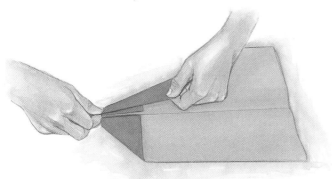

4 Fold the corners into the middle as shown.

5 Now fold the sides into the middle. Cut off the ends.

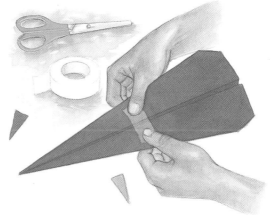

6 Turn the dart over. Fold the sides together. Pull out the sides to make the wings. Tape the top of the wings together.

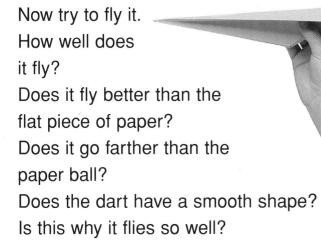

Now try to fly it.
How well does it fly?
Does it fly better than the flat piece of paper?
Does it go farther than the paper ball?
Does the dart have a smooth shape?
Is this why it flies so well?

Air Lift

When you pump up a tire you push air into it. The air is squashed into a small space. Squashed, or **compressed**, air is very strong.

Blow power

1 Put two books on a table. Bend down in front of them and blow. They don't move, do they?

2 Put the books on a large plastic bag on a table.

3 Gather the opening of the bag and tie loosely with string. Put in a straw. Blow through the straw into the bag. What is lifting the books? It is compressed air.

Float away

Let's see which **parachute** takes the longest time to fall.

1 Cut out two large newspaper and plastic circles.

2 Cut six pieces of string 8 in. (20 cm) long. Tape them around the edge of a paper circle. Tie a small bead to the other ends of the strings. Tie the beads together. Do the same with a plastic circle.

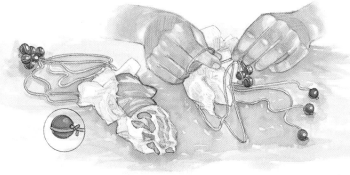

3 Crumple the other two circles into balls. Attach strings and beads in the same way.

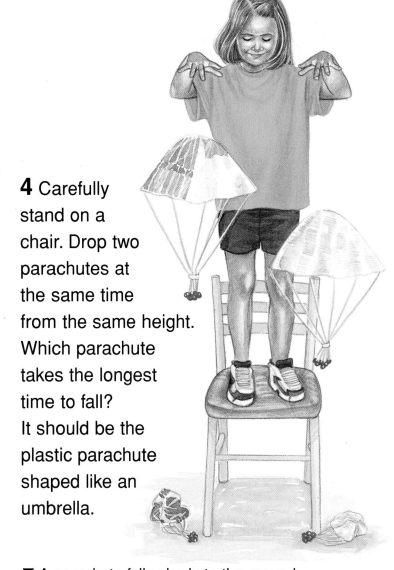

4 Carefully stand on a chair. Drop two parachutes at the same time from the same height. Which parachute takes the longest time to fall? It should be the plastic parachute shaped like an umbrella.

▼ A parachute falls slowly to the ground because air is trapped inside it.

Windy Weather

When air moves outside, it makes the **wind**. The wind can blow from any place. It can blow hard or gently.

Look at this picture. What is causing the streamers to move? Is the wind blowing hard?

Which way?

We can make a wind vane to find out which way the wind is blowing.

1 Draw a cross on top of a plastic container. Write N, S, E, and W on four sticky labels. Stick them on your pot at the ends of the cross.

2 Make a hole through the middle of the cross. Push in a thin stick. Make sure it is upright. Tape the container to a plastic tray.

3 Draw an arrow on stiff cardboard. Cut it out. Tape it to the top of an old pen lid. Make sure the arrow is straight.

4 Put the arrow holder on top of the stick. Make sure it can turn easily.

5 Take your wind vane outside. Put it on a chair. Use a compass to find where north is. Put your wind vane so that the N is pointing north. Does the arrow move when it is windy? The arrow points in the direction the wind is blowing. So a southerly wind makes the arrow point northward.

Wind Power

The wind can be caught and used to push things. It can push boats along. It can drive machines such as windmills.

Sail away

1 Cut a square of paper. Tape it to one end of a straw. This is your sail.

3 Attach the sail to the middle of a small plastic box or lid. Press the modeling clay down hard.

2 Put some modeling clay on the other end of the straw.

4 Put your boat into a bowl of water. Blow gently into the sail. What happens? The boat is pushed along. Try larger and smaller sails. Which make the boat sail best?

Windmill

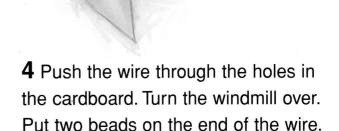

1 Make a hole in the middle of a piece of cardboard, 8 in. (20 cm) square. Draw lines from the corners almost to the center. Cut along the lines. Put stars in the corners as shown.

2 Ask an adult to help you. Make a hole in each star. Fold these corners into the middle. They should overlap.

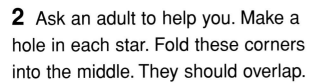

3 Push a bead onto a piece of stiff, plastic-covered wire. Bend the wire over the bead. Twist the ends together.

4 Push the wire through the holes in the cardboard. Turn the windmill over. Put two beads on the end of the wire.

5 Make a hole near the top of a straw. Push the wire through the hole. Make sure the wire is straight.

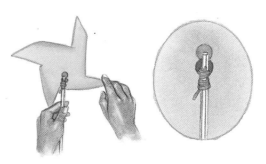

6 Make sure the windmill can turn. Twist the wire tightly around the straw.

Gently blow on the windmill. What happens? The wind makes the windmill spin.

Materials You Will Need

p. 6 Air? Where?—sheet of paper, tape, or stapler, bottle, bowl, water.

p. 8 Weigh It Up—balloons, balloon pump, long stick, felt-tipped pen, ruler, string, tape, round-ended scissors.

p. 10 Air Power—ruler, large sheet of paper, two drinking glasses, cling film, tape, a straw, box, round-ended scissors, washable felt-tipped pen, cardboard.

p. 12 Up, Up, and Away—balloon, plastic bottle, large bowl, warm water, ice, thread, a straw, colored pencils or washable felt-tipped pens, round-ended scissors, tape. You will need to hang something over a warm radiator.

p. 14 Keep Warm—five jars of the same size, woolen scarf, box, newspapers or scrap paper, sheet of thick paper, tape, round-ended scissors, thick plastic, very warm water.

p. 16 On the Move—two books, large sheet of paper, two small plastic bricks, string, sticky tape, round-ended scissors.

p. 18 Up We Go—tissue paper, ruler, round-ended scissors, tape.

p. 20 Let's Fly—three pieces of paper 8$\frac{1}{2}$ in. X 11 in. (21$\frac{1}{2}$ cm X 28 cm), round-ended scissors, tape.

p. 22 Air Lift—two thin books, large plastic bag, a straw, newspaper, large sheet of plastic, round-ended scissors, string, tape, small beads, chair.

p. 24 Windy Weather—washable felt-tipped pen, four sticky labels, clean plastic container, a drawing pin to make a hole in the bottom of the container, thin stick, tape, plastic tray, stiff cardboard, round-ended scissors, ruler, old pen lid, chair, a compass to find where north is.

p. 26 Wind Power—paper, round-ended scissors, straws, tape, modeling clay, small plastic box or lid, bowl, water, cardboard 8 in. (20 cm) square, ruler, pencil, four sticky stars, small beads, stiff plastic-covered wire. You will need a drawing pin to make holes in the cardboard and the straw.

Hints to Helpers

Pages 6 and 7

Discuss why you can feel moving air and not still air. The still air is pressing evenly on your body. Many solid things have air trapped inside them. Try putting a handful of soil into water and watch the bubbles come out. Put a small unbaked clay brick in water and see the air bubbles rise. Leave a glass of water and see the bubbles gather on the inside of the glass.

Page 9

It is very important that the balloons weigh the same. One balloon should be blown up as much as possible and stuck back in the same place. You could ask what would happen if the balloon burst. Discuss where the air would go and what would happen to the stick. Burst the balloon to confirm that the weight of the balloon was due to the air and that the stick would balance again and lie level.

Pages 10 and 11

The sheet of paper should be large, as shown in the photograph. The ruler should be hit sharply but not too hard. (If you press down on the ruler, it will act as a lever and lift the paper.) Most children expect the paper to fly into the air, but the air pressing down on the paper keeps the paper and ruler from moving.

The plastic wrap must be tightly stretched over the top of the glass to make a flexible membrane. When the atmospheric pressure is high, the outside air presses down harder on the plastic wrap, so the plastic wrap dips down and the pointer rises. When the air pressure is lower, the outside air does not press down as much on the plastic wrap. The air inside the glass pushes the plastic wrap up, so the pointer goes down. The cardboard rule should have divisions marked on it. The movement of the marker will be very slight.

Pages 12 and 13

Look at pictures of hot-air balloons and birds circling in thermals. Discuss how the hot air rising is used to help hot-air balloons, gliders, and birds rise into the air.

Pages 14 and 15

Discuss how we use insulation in the home. Talk about warm clothes in cold weather and how it is better to wear two or three layers of clothes with air trapped in between than one very thick layer. Discuss how comforters, which have lots of air trapped in the feathers or fibers, keep you warm in bed.

Pages 16 and 17

Moving air has less pushing power than still air. So when you blow beneath the paper instead of flying away, the paper dips because the air pressure on top is pushing it down.

Similarly, the air moving between the bricks has less pushing power than the still air at the side of the bricks, so the still air pushes the bricks together. The same effect is seen in whirlwinds. The air pressure in the center is lower than the air pressure outside the whirlwind. Therefore, objects in the high-pressure area are pushed into the low-pressure area in the moving column of air.

Pages 18 and 19

The air moves faster over the curved top surface of the paper wing than beneath the wing. The air pressure above the wing is lower and has less pushing power. The higher air pressure below the paper wing pushes it up into the air. The straight wing does not rise up when you blow. Air flows over and beneath the wing at the same speed. The air pressure above and beneath the wing is equal, so the wing does not rise.

Pages 20 and 21

Discuss the shape of aircraft and gliders. Look at pictures of the first aircraft and modern fast-flying planes such as jets. Compare them with the shape of the dart. Discuss how you could make the dart better, e.g., bending the wings up. Try different sizes of darts with longer and shorter wings; try a different dart shape, e.g., with a long nose.

Page 23

When a parachute falls, air is trapped and compressed inside the bell shape. Therefore, the air pressure inside the parachute is higher and pushes it up. The push is not great enough to overcome the pull of gravity, but it is enough to slow the fall of the parachute. Try making different shaped parachutes and see which one takes the longest to fall.

Pages 24 and 25

Explain the positions of north, south, east, and west on a compass.

Discuss windy weather and how the wind moves at different speeds. Winds blow from areas of high air pressure to areas of low pressure. Very strong winds and hurricanes are caused by a great difference in air pressure. Winds are always given as the direction they come from, so a northerly wind is blowing from the north to the south.

Look at books on the weather. Talk about weather forecasts and wind direction. For example, in the winter southwesterly winds often bring rain, and easterly winds often bring cold, fine weather, or snow.

Pages 26 and 27

Look at pictures of windmills and boats. Discuss how the shape of the sails helps catch the wind. Make a simple boat and try different shaped sails. See which work best, and make the boat move fastest when you sail them.

Glossary

Air pressure The pressure of the air all around us. It presses down on everything on Earth. You cannot usually feel this pressure on you. This is because there is equal air pressure inside your body pushing outward.

Compressed This means that something is squashed into a small space. When air is compressed it is very strong. Compressed air is strong enough to power drills that break up concrete.

Contracts Gets smaller. Lots of things such as air and metal contract when they are cooled.

Deflates Gets smaller as gas or air is released. A blown-up balloon deflates when you let air out of it.

Expands Swells out or increases in size. Lots of things such as air, metal and water expand when they are warmed.

Gravity The pulling force that draws objects toward the center of the earth. Gravity keeps everything on Earth from flying off into space. It also makes objects have a weight.

Inflates Gets bigger by being filled with gas or air. A balloon inflates when you blow air into it.

Insulation A layer of material around an object that heat cannot pass through easily. It keeps the object hot or cold for longer.

Parachute A large piece of fabric attached to strings that can be worn by a person. It slows down the fall of the person jumping from an aircraft.

Streamlined A smooth shape that allows air or a liquid to flow around it easily.

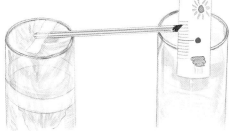

Weather Day-to-day temperature (if it's hot or cold), rain, cloud, and wind in a place.

Whirlwind A column of fast-moving air that whirls around and moves over the land or sea.

Wind Air that flows from places with high air pressure to places with low air pressure.

Further reading

Branley, Franklyn. *Air Is All Around You* (Let's Read and Find Out Science). New York: HarperCollins, 1986.

Charman, Andrew. *Air* (First Starts). Austin, TX: Raintree Steck-Vaughn, 1994.

Murphy, Bryan. *Experiment with Air* (Experiment With). Minneapolis, MN: Lerner Publications, 1992.

Robbins, Kenn. *Air: The Elements*. New York: Henry Holt, 1995.

White, Larry. *Air: Simple Experiments for Young Scientists*. Brookfield, CT: Millbrook Press, 1996.

Index

© Copyright 1998 Wayland (Publishers) Ltd.